PRAISE FOR
THE RECOGNITON BOOK

Published by
LID Publishing Limited
The Record Hall, Studio 204,
16-16a Baldwins Gardens,
London EC1N 7RJ, UK

524 Broadway, 11th Floor, Suite 08-120,
New York, NY 10012, US

info@lidpublishing.com
www.lidpublishing.com

A member of:

www.businesspublishersroundtable.com

© Paul F. Warriner, 2019
© LID Publishing Limited, 2019
Reprinted in 2019

Printed in Latvia by Jelgavas Tipogrāfija

ISBN: 978-1-911498-88-9

Cover and page design: Matthew Renaudin

THE RECOGNITION BOOK

50 WAYS TO STEP UP, STAND OUT AND GET RECOGNIZED

PAUL F. WARRINER

LONDON   NEW YORK   BOGOTA
MADRID   BARCELONA   BUENOS AIRES
MEXICO CITY   MONTERREY   SHANGHAI

FOR OTHER TITLES
IN THE SERIES...

CONCISE ADVICE LAB

SMALL BOOKS: BIG IDEAS

CONTENTS

ACKNOWLEDGMENTS

They say that there is a book inside all of us, well this one took some teasing out! I would like to thank all of these people for their encouragement and faith.

Firstly Chris West who worked at Brita, who sadly passed away a few years ago but provided the initial inspiration for this book. This book is dedicated to her.

Then Yana Maksimochkina for hearing my thoughts and all the team at LID Publishing for their professional support and assistance, Nikki Mullin, Sara Taheri and Martin Liu.

Professor Chris Brady, Rene Carayol and Melanie Williams for showing me the way.

My family, friends and colleagues for their enthusiasm and unwavering belief in me throughout.

And of course all the clients, teachers, coaches and people I have had the privilege to work with over the years and from whom I have learned so much; Simon Fletcher, Kevan Stirrat, Joseph Rachel, Paul Hoddinot to name a few.

I know there will be many I have failed to recognize in this acknowledgement section, ironic really considering the title of the book! I thank you all from the bottom of my heart and I look forward to hearing your feedback.

INTRODUCTION

WHAT DOES RECOGNITION MEAN TO YOU?

This book is about recognition, or rather how to step up and get the recognition you deserve.

In this context, recognition means: appreciation or acclaim for an achievement, service, or ability.

Recognition comes from the Latin verb *recognoscere* 'know again, recall to mind'.

But what does recognition mean to you?

Is it a higher salary? Is it promotion? Is it the opportunity to do something new or is it just a smile, or a thank you?

Whatever it is, financial or otherwise, it's fair to say that we all want it sometimes. It can be an elusive element of our working lives.

So, this book really focuses on the workplace but many of the principles and ideas can equally be applied to other parts of your life: family, community even spiritual.

Recognition has the power to lift your spirits, change your attitude, fill you with a newborn energy, change your outlook and transform your life.

The right kind of recognition, the one you want, will help you move mountains and achieve anything you set your mind to.

So where to start ...

With this statement: "Everyone deserves to be recognized."

If, like me, you believe that we all need recognition and that this nourishes the soul, then you'll agree that Spencer Johnson and Kenneth Blanchard were right to state that "Feedback is the breakfast of champions," in their book *The One Minute Manager.*

To be a champion, to stand out, to be the best in your field, there are many elements to consider, but feedback and recognition are definitely two of them.

To the sprinter, the clock is feedback, the medals the recognition. To the rock star, the applause, the cheers, the hysteria, the encores are feedback, the continuing sold-out stadiums show the recognition.

And to the tireless accounts clerk, the balanced ledger is the feedback and the paid invoice and replaced order shows recognition!

That's the point of this book. What do you want as recognition? What does your employer give as feedback and recognition?

To get what you want and deserve, read on.

HAVE YOU CHOSEN WELL?

It's tough to get the recognition you deserve when you're doing something you don't like. It's not impossible, but it is tough to keep it up.

That's why choosing the right job is ultimately so important. I say ultimately because using the principle that "if a job is worth doing well, it's worth doing poorly at first", we all need to practice until we have mastered the job.

Anecdotal evidence suggests that over 50% of UK workers are in the wrong career. While this sounds frustrating if you are one of the individuals in this position, it's also a great opportunity to practise the principles presented in this book.

Don't be despondent with your first few career choices, and make sure that you have a plan. A plan to find and earn a living in a career that you love.

A plan well practiced will build competence, competence will build confidence and confidence will build the courage you need to move to do the job that is perfect for you. And therefore to get the recognition that you deserve.

Career planning is such an important factor for your success that it truly warrants a book of its own.

PLAY AS IF 'A SCOUT' IS WATCHING

Many years ago, when I was at school in Nottingham, an old physical education (PE) teacher of mine gave me this piece of advice:

"Whenever you are out there on the pitch, play every second as if a scout is watching." He said the same to me whether it was football, rugby, tennis or even swimming. I suppose he said the same to all the other kids. I was not strong at football or rugby, but some went on to play for their county.

I did, however, reach a very high national level at swimming, thanks in part to my PE teacher, and his constant encouragement.

I guess, in a roundabout way, what my PE teacher was really saying was to always try hard, do your best, play all-out, leave nothing on the pitch. You have probably heard many of these and plenty of other similar phrases.

They translate perfectly well to the workplace. You never know who is watching, who is making judgments, based on a momentary glimpse of a random piece of work.

If you approached all your work as if the "boss was watching" then surely you would get the recognition you deserve?

Well to ensure you do, keep reading because cracking 'The Recognition Code' may not be as simple as it sounds!

A couple of points to keep in mind when reading this book. The first is that there is no timescale that you need to stick to. To get the recognition that you want could happen in a moment, or could be part of a longer plan, a few months, maybe even years. It will depend on your plan, the environment, the systems and the processes. What's important is that you know where you are.

The second is that this book is designed to be a reference guide for everyone, so it doesn't matter if you are a newbie or a seasoned executive. As you progress through the book and develop your recognition skills, you may find yourself dipping back to remind yourself of ideas and points that seem much more relevant than they did before.

Each time you re-read something, its meaning and relevance may change, because your understanding, behaviours and skills in getting recognition will be changing and advancing.

Enjoy this journey, take notes, keep a journal, record the recognition that you start to receive, as you truly deserve it.

KNOW WHO YOU ARE

The first step in this journey is to learn and find out about yourself. You have to get to know yourself really well. This isn't just dipping and peeking. What I am suggesting is to take a deep dive and a really good look around inside. Get a map of the territory.

Have you ever taken a psychometric test? There are many out there. Some are free, others you pay for, some are online, some are in hard copy, some are complex whilst others are simple. Your company may use them during their recruitment processes, and so they should: these tests are a great baseline to work from.

Taking a psychometric test is a brave first step to take, but it shows intent. Usually the results are instant, and they will surprise you. The results may even make you question the validity of the test. But, if it's a well-recognized psychometric system, you must have trust, just take a deep breath and read on. Try to look beyond the words and understand what the results are showing, the perception of who you are and what you are like.

Even if you find that you disagree with some of the results, take them as a starting point and something to build from. Often the results show what you intuitively know about yourself, but may find hard to admit.

What's your intuition? It's that little all-knowing voice inside your head, it's that gut feeling, you know the one! The one you wish you had trusted before you bought that shirt!

It's our sixth sense and arguably the most powerful. It's not used much, and is under-developed in most people, but it's there. Because we operate in the physical world, our physical senses tend to lead the way. But have you ever walked into a room and sensed an atmosphere? That is your intuition.

The more you develop and use your intuition, the stronger it will become. You will get a feeling about your job, your boss, your company. Pay attention to these signals: they are there for a reason.

To help you understand a little more about who you are, use the questions below to start this journey of discovery.

1. **What are your core values?**
2. **What are your beliefs?**
3. **What do you like about yourself?**
4. **What would you change?**
5. **What one possession would you rescue if your house were on fire?**

This journey that starts here may take a lifetime to work out. Starting it is the important thing. Knowing who you truly are will help you get what you really want, and that is our next step.

KNOW WHAT YOU WANT

This is one of the hardest things to pin down. You may know what you like, but actually what you really want can be more difficult to identify. There is so much choice in all areas, so much information to help you make decisions, and so many advisors to listen to.

You may want a new home, but where? How much bigger is big enough? You may want a new car, but which one, what criteria should you use? Do you go with your heart or your head? Or you may want a new job, but doing what? Often, it's easier to say what you *don't* want rather than putting in the effort to think hard and define what you really *do* want.

Perhaps that is why you settle for what you have, settling for what you know is easily achievable. Drifting aimlessly along and then one day waking up and asking: "how did I end up here?"

Most people have hopes, dreams and aspirations, but never quite formulate them into goals. And even fewer write them down. People tend to set their sights on what they know they can achieve. Occasionally, they stretch to what they think can be done, but hardly ever do they reach for what will truly change them.

This is why individuals that succeed in identifying their goals with a plan of action on how to achieve them outperform those who do not.

In the context of your work, the right career path is where you need to put in the hard yards. Spending time on this, thinking, planning, preparing, comparing, even experimenting, are vital.

The effort in identifying the best career path will pay dividends. You often hear people say "do what you love," "follow your passion and it won't seem like work."

To help you to start to think about what your passion is, here are a few questions to consider:

1. **If you knew you couldn't fail, what is the one thing that you would do?**
2. **If you had all the money you needed, what would you do with your time?**
3. **What activity gives you the greatest buzz?**
4. **If you had six months to live, how would you spend it?**

These are just a few questions, but you get the point. Use them to help you define what is the ideal career for you.

Today we are lucky in that if the ideal role doesn't exist, we can often create it. Technology and a global market make all things possible.

Living the dream is entirely possible if only you can dream it.

KNOW WHERE AND WHAT YOU WANT TO BE RECOGNIZED FOR

It's all about you. All about who you are, deep down inside, your values, your beliefs, your passions, desires and how you want to be recognized and remembered.

This is where we introduce the concept of 'the recognition plan'. It's similar to a business plan, it's where you lay out the roadmap for your recognition journey. It needs to cover a long enough time frame so that you can measure your progress. Of course, you should have Key Performance Indicators (KPIs) and milestones, but it's your plan, so write it your way.

To start your recognition plan, you need to define your vision. Your goal. Where in your career do you want to be recognized, for what do you want to be recognized and what does that recognition look like? This is also where you set the timeframe for your plan.

Don't forget: it could be just a smile or a 'thank you.' It doesn't have to be a global achievement award for services rendered.

Once your vision and goals are set out, you need to understand **how you are**, now. Then note how you would like to be in the future. For example, what character traits do you have now and which ones would serve you better in getting the recognition you want?

For the second part of the recognition plan think about **how you treat others**? Where are you today, and where would you like to be down the road?

An important point is that when preparing a recognition plan, it doesn't matter where you start. You could be starting your first job or starting your first board appointment. The timeframe you set for reaching your recognition goals could be one day, one week, a month, a year, three years, or a lifetime. Your recognition goals could be task driven, project driven or even departmental. The point is you create a recognition plan with thought and care, review it regularly and record the progress and outcomes.

For the third section of the plan, you need to think about **what it is that you do**. What do you do now and what is it that you need to do to get the recognition you think you want? Some of these things will be activity-based and some will be developmental.

The fourth section of your plan will be focusing on **how you behave**, now and going forward. What are the behaviours you need to start demonstrating in order to be recognized?

So, let's begin preparing a recognition plan.

At each stage leave space for notes, to monitor the feedback and record the results you are or are not getting. If through the course of the plan you find something isn't working, simply tweak it. Constantly appraise the results and make sure you do what it takes to keep you moving towards your goals.

A great addition to the recognition plan is a recognition card. This is a business-card sized reminder that you can carry around with you with a summary of the main points of your recognition plan. You can refer to it frequently during the day as a constant reminder of your plan.

Start your plan by thinking about and developing your goals. Refer to the section later on in the book on goal setting. Once you have worked out what you want to achieve, the template below will help you focus on the actions needed to get you there.

RECOGNITION PLAN
TEMPLATE

Section	Where are you now?	Where do you want to be?	What will you do?
1 How You Are			
2 How You Treat Others			
3 What You Do			
4 How You Behave			

KNOW WHO YOU ARE, HOW YOU ARE

In this section, we will take a look at some of the values and character traits that can help people get recognition. It is not an extensive list by any means: there are many more. It's important to note, that as well as the traits mentioned here, there are negative character traits that could definitely get you noticed for the wrong reasons, but we have not focused on these either.

Reading about some of the key characteristics, you will become familiar in how to approach, interrogate and query your traits, think about how they are different, and whether they help or hinder you in your quest for recognition.

1. ENTHUSIASM

So much has been written about this and most of it true. Do I really need to mention it? Yes.

Enthusiasm is a key ingredient to being successful in all kinds of things. Getting the recognition you think you deserve will undoubtedly require you to be enthusiastic most of the time, if not all of the time.

Being enthusiastic and keen in a new job may not be too difficult initially. The urge to make a good impression may be easy to muster. Staying enthusiastic, and wanting to please all the time, is a lot more challenging.

How do you do it?

Dale Carnegie summed it up well when he used this phrase in his training sessions: "Act enthusiastic and you'll be enthusiastic." This works for sustaining your keen appetite and finding it for tasks and projects you don't enjoy. Because these will come!

It's a lot to do. But with the right mindset, the right physiology, the right game plan you can do it. In order to maintain the required enthusiasm to see the job through, you will need to have a goal, to see the end result and understand your purpose.

How do athletes keep doing the same old boring 'reps' every day, every week? Because they have the end in mind.

Not only is enthusiasm unstoppable, it's also contagious. Getting people to come along with you on this journey is a surefire way to get the recognition you think you deserve.

An enthusiastic attitude can highlight mediocrity and complacency, two qualities that need to be avoided when embarking on a recognition journey.

2. POSITIVITY

What can I say? Does this really get you recognition? Does it make a good impression if you have a positive outlook? If you have a 'can do attitude' does it make a difference?

What do you think? This could be the shortest section of the book!

Naturally, being positive makes a difference, it matters, it gets you recognized. And I literally mean: **Naturally**.

There is a lot of information that supports the idea of the power of being positive. People are attracted to positive people, positive people magnetize an area and have the ability to lift and inspire others.

If you are one of these people, carry on, work hard to maintain your positive attitude: it will serve you well.

But if your cup is half empty, if there is no silver lining or the seed of positivity, if it is difficult to see, let alone sow, then what can you do?

There is a lot out there that can help and guide you. In the first instance, you should make a deliberate attempt to find out what works for you, try not reading the papers, watching the news, or if possible try not watching TV! Instead, start by drinking more water, meditating, practicing mindfulness.

Positivity is about awareness, self-awareness. The key is to accept who you are and surround yourself with positive people, remembering that a positive person will be recognized by their peers and employers.

3. HUMILITY

A sense of self-awareness can bring with it a sense of humility. When you are humble, you appreciate where you come from, you have the ability to reflect on your journey and look to help others on theirs.

We all make mistakes. These mistakes give us experience and help us to make decisions to get us to where we want to be.

Through humility and learning from our own mistakes, we can help others learn and shorten their journey to where they want to be. This alone is the recognition that each mistake, each apparent failure, each interaction is a learning opportunity and will be of huge value to us and others.

Being humble is not a weakness; neither is it a submissive character trait. It is a deep understanding of our own fallibility, allowing people to connect and warm to you. That brings with it a special kind of recognition.

4. COURAGE

"Fortune favours the brave."

"He who dares wins."

Words you will have heard plenty times. Risks are around us everywhere. Knowing which ones to take and which ones to ignore requires good judgment.

Crossing the road is dangerous. With care and practice we can master this. We learn what roads we can cross, where to cross, how to judge the speed of the approaching traffic and how assess the associated risks around us.

But we don't just dive into this activity. Someone holds our hand, helps us to get started and shows us the way. There are even professional advisers in special places to ensure we survive. Eventually, through successful repetition, we venture out on our own, sometimes under the watchful eye of an interested party, but we feel capable of doing this.

As with most things, there is a starting point, an objective and a technique, which is either good or bad, but probably could be improved upon.

So why don't we apply this tried and tested system to other forms of risk? Every working day, opportunities for advancement are presented, to move your position forward. Taking action can be difficult, because in order to be courageous, you may have to put your comfort at risk.

Being courageous takes judgment and a plan to follow. So, courage without judgment is folly. And it usually doesn't end well.

Having a plan, a vision of the outcome in mind, will be your reference point when you are being courageous. If you can rehearse, then find the time. It will pay you dividends. People think they can tackle new, difficult situations on the 'fly'. Trust me, the outcomes will improve significantly if you have a plan and stick to it.

Remember the first time you asked someone out on a date? Were you nervous? Did you fear rejection? Was there a lot at stake? Could your whole world be shattered if it backfired? Did you spend days planning what you were going to say, where it would happen, considering all the possible outcomes?

This mental role play is normal: we all do it, but not in all circumstances. Why not? If it is important, it is important to prepare, and prepare well.

Unwavering courage draws the best out of us. You have to be able to step up and bet on yourself. Your judgment will improve the more you practice. The more you practice, the easier it will be to take action. And the more you take action, the more courageous you will feel and the more you will get out of life.

Be more chicken and cross more roads!

Being brave and taking more risks to further your career will get you recognized.

5. CURIOSITY

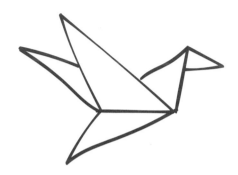

A few years ago, I started an informal gathering called the 'Curiosity Club'. We would meet, usually in a pub, and discuss things that interested us. We wanted to know why things were the were the way they were. We weren't people of science so I am sure things could have been explained a lot more easily than we could.

We considered questions like "why is space black?" and "how do Cuckoo chicks get away with it?" You can see the level I am talking about. I am sure all great thinkers started small like this and gradually built up to address more of the challenging issues of the time.

Curiously, the group didn't last long. I wonder why? It probably ran out of energy. Perhaps we didn't ask the right questions that stimulated us. Perhaps we felt "why bother, we can't change things anyway!"

Looking back, these are telling revelations that apply to a lot of situations. Things grow where our attention goes. To give life to something takes energy. To improve things requires better-quality questioning. To come up with better-quality questions takes curiosity and a desire to improve and grow.

Curiosity leads to problem-solving on a whole new level. Being able to solve our problems will certainly get you recognition.

'Why,' is a very simple question. One we master at a very early age. But for some reason we stop asking. If you don't ask that killer question the world does not change. In sales, if you don't ask for 'the order' you won't get it.

There are many questions to ask and many ways to ask them: at least be curious about this.

Your curiosity will lead you to experience whole new worlds where recognition could be commonplace.

6. AMBITION

Ambition is one of those obvious character traits that is the cornerstone of all recognition. In fact, it is so obvious that I nearly forgot to mention it. Sometimes the obvious is hidden in plain sight and gets missed.

Couple this with determination and a single-minded approach and you will not stop until you stand on top of that podium and on the front cover.

Behind every champion, there is a drive and ambition that keeps them going through thick and thin. Win, lose or draw, they look for the positives, the takeaways they can use to improve and do better.

The spark that started the desire to do something is fueled by ambition and drive for recognition.

We are all born with gifts for something special. Our duty to the world is to find out what that gift is, develop it and share it. Often our ambitions are not realized because we have not identified our gifts.

As with a lot of our character traits, they are buried deep inside us and all too often we look outward for solutions and answers, when really the doors to these treasures open inwards.

Find your gifts and you will have the ambition to give them away.

7. STRENGTHS

Playing to your strengths is a much better strategy to get ahead, and it is definitely more effective than focusing on your weaknesses.

Knowing your strengths is the starting point.

- **What do you love to do?**
- **What makes you feel good?**
- **What gives you a real buzz?**
- **What do you do that makes time fly?**
- **When do you feel invincible?**
- **What were you doing the last time positive things just flowed your way?**

In answering these questions, look forward and see if you would be a better person if you were doing more of this stuff. Would you feel happier, have more fun, feel less stressed and able to cope with more of what the world has to offer?

If the answer is "yes" or close enough, then dig deep and find that courage to make a change. Playing small does not serve the world. It is our duty to be fully out there, giving it our best shot.

Knowing your strengths, playing to them and then mastering them can give you the recognition you want. Being a specialist in something earns more recognition than being a generalist. Loving one person deeply can be more satisfying than knowing a lot. The cumulative energy is unstoppable.

Know your strengths and master them. Look to partner with other people that have complementary strengths. Build a team, a board, a department that demonstrates the key strengths of each member.

Spend more time in the zone. Look to develop your strengths so that these help improve your performance and inspire others to reach for new heights so that they too can be recognized.

8. CREATIVITY

Creativity is one of these gifts. We are all creative. We all have imaginations and use them to some degree or other. We can all conjure up positive or negative thoughts.

Everything that mankind has invented is a product of our imagination and our creativity.

You don't have to be painter or a writer or craft anything in particular to be creative. Just close your eyes and think, just shut off that internal chatter and you are being creative, you are controlling the flow of conscious thought. Go with this long enough and magic will happen.

Like curiosity, the ability to ask a better question will lead you in joining the dots that you didn't see before, and this will lead to creating a new picture.

"You never change things by fighting the existing reality. To change something, build a new model that makes the existing model obsolete." **Buckminster Fuller**

This doesn't need to be a life-changing action; it could be a new way to process an order within the sales department.

The original thought that leads to this change is the creative force for improvement. Continue this in all that you do, and you will have the recognition that you deserve.

RECOGNITION PLAN
SECTION ONE

Now that you have looked at how you are, it is time to start your recognition plan. Perhaps the hardest section of all is to examine who you are deep down. This is extremely important, so take your time and reflect.

Section	Where are you now?	Where do you want to be?	What will you do?
1 How You Are	Enthusiastic Cynical	Be seen to be enthusiastic Adopt a more positive approach	Speak up at the next team meeting about my new productivity idea Talk with colleagues about what is going well
2 How You Treat Others			
3 What You Do			
4 How You Behave			

HOW YOU
TREAT OTHERS

In this section, we highlight and discuss some of the ways
you can positively treat people to enhance your relationships
and get recognized for being the person you are,
or the person you want to become.

Once again, it is not an exhaustive list, but you will find the
points raised useful and the insights valuable in determining
how these affect your success in getting recognized.

9. LISTENING

This is definitely an active past time. A key skill that seems to be disappearing from everybody's kit bag.

According to Stephen Covey: "Most people don't listen with the intent to understand: they listen with the intent to reply."

How true that is.

We may pick up on a few words and formulate our response, then fire it back without even trying to understand or process the other person's comments. This is when you get the talking-over situation, when two or three people are trying to get a point across, each getting louder and louder trying to be heard and appearing to know it all. No-one is hearing the full statement or even caring!

This is so common. Perhaps this is why we answer our own questions, often guessing what others would have said and saying it for them. Using pre-positioning statements like "I know what you are going to say ... but ...", or "you're not going to like this, but ...".

You may have heard the saying, "We have two ears and one mouth, we should use them in that proportion." There is potentially so much that we miss when we don't actively listen. Active listening requires energy, patience, intent, understanding, compassion and interest. And an underlying interest in broadening your own perspective.

When you are listening to something, your brain is automatically filtering out the background noise so you can listen to what is important. Naturally, you will then add your own ego filters on top and filter out anything that doesn't fit with your biases.

The human spirit is all for expansion and growth and on a daily basis we limit this. When someone is speaking to you, pay attention to every word, all the nuances they use, the inflections, the speed, the tone, the volume, the non-verbal signals that accompany the conversation. Even what they repeat. If you talk to people on the phone, you have to work extra hard on what you can hear, because that's all you have to go on.

That is why it's necessary to pay attention. There is so much to gain from listening with intent. Because good listening requires energy and commitment. And this investment is well worth it. Its return will serve you well. It will definitely get you recognized.

Have you ever been to an event, spoken with someone new, they politely listened, you parted company and you thought "weren't they a nice person?"

Imagine this the other way around. What impact could you make if you just politely listened?

10. BLAMING

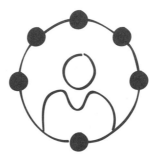

The blame culture seems to be everywhere. "It's not my fault it's ..."

Here you could fill in the blanks. The economy, management, the company, the competition, my age, my gender, the industry I am in, my friendship group, my boss, timing.

Virtually everything can be blamed for something happening to you, or not happening to you.

It's very rarely seen as something that we have done, a decision we have made or something that we can do something about.

This tendency to blame sits hand in hand with the reluctance to take 100% responsibility for the results you get and for all that happens to you.

This may not prevent some of the events that happen, but it will affect how you respond, how you look to fix it and make the best of the situation.

Always look for the good in something. As Napoleon Hill said in his book *Think and Grow Rich,* "Every adversity, every failure, every heartache carries with it the seed of an equal or greater benefit."

One of Denis Waitley's favourite sayings was: "Things turn out best in life for those who make the best of how things turn out."

Wise words from two great authors.

What can you do to change the circumstances you are blaming? Can you speak to someone, change your strategy, change your attitude, change your job, change the direction you are heading and follow your passion?

Blaming a circumstance or someone else takes away your personal power, your control. Taking it back will free you up to do more, to explore more options to be recognized for who you really are and progress to who you can become.

Tweaking your approach can have a large impact. It's all about taking responsibility, so you may consider starting earlier or finishing later, preparing for that meeting instead of just turning up, speaking up when asked if you have any comments, making that call or actually reading that report everybody has been talking about.

You must keep in mind that if you're not working to a plan, you're probably part of someone else's. So, don't blame others because they have a plan: get your own.

11. COMPASSION

To show deep understanding is a fantastic character trait. Not a sign of weakness, but a sign of strength and awareness of the people you work with.

To be recognized for being compassionate would be a great achievement and one that only a few attain. It takes time, patience and desire to put yourself in others people's shoes, to see things from their perspective and understand their viewpoint.

"To first buy what John Smith buys you must first see John Smith through John Smith's eyes." This is a quote I learned many years ago on a sales training course. It's only now that I see its true value. Being John Smith for that moment takes an extraordinary amount of insight. Not guess work, because being John Smith in that moment is the only way to get the result.

It is valuable to be able to step outside your own ego for a moment and see things from a different standpoint. Interpreting compassion this way will get you noticed and give you a greater sense of the impact you have in the work that you do. Apply this principle to getting the recognition you think you deserve. What does your current situation look like? Whose viewpoint do you need to achieve the result you want?

Compassion also means kindness. When was the last time you showed genuine kindness to someone at work? Or anywhere? Not just doing something because it's convenient or routine, but because you really felt like doing it.

To show this level of kindness, you must first show a level of interest that is rare in today's fast-paced, self-absorbed world. Compassion takes time and commitment, but like any skill, the more you do it, the easier it becomes. With time, you will find it easier to spot opportunities to act in a different way, to go out of your way to be kind, considerate and compassionate to others.

To be recognized for being compassionate, kind and thoughtful, you must first recognize the need, seize the opportunity and take action. You will also have elevated yourself to a completely new level, a level few people reach, and you won't be the only person glad that you did.

12. BEING HELPFUL

So basic, so simple. Just find the time. Or to be really helpful, plan the time. Like any great show or event that looks spontaneous, it's meticulously planned and rehearsed. Down to the last detail, all eventualities are considered.

It's the same with helping someone. You probably know what they need help with, so plan ahead, schedule the time to do so, on your own terms. Make it part of your plan to be helpful. Take an interest in everyone, they will thank you for it in many ways. And a thank you is recognition.

Cast your mind back to school to who was your favourite teacher? Probably the one whose lessons were interesting, where you could ask questions without being judged and where the teacher always had time for you, in or out of the classroom.

Try to be remembered for your willingness to help: being remembered this way is recognition.

13. RESPECT

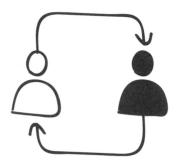

Hand in hand with being compassionate is showing respect. No matter what the situation, your mood, or the occasion, maintaining your respect for others is vital.

Many people spend their whole working life wanting respect from others, under the illusion that their rank or position automatically carries with it respect.

We are taught at a very early age to respect our elders. Why? We are told to respect authority but why, when they may not represent our view? Our parents, the church, the police, teachers, doctors, our fellow man, everyone seems to be on the watch list! But why?

These are great questions that you may have asked yourself.

Has anyone ever told you what respect means, how you earn it and keep it? Take a few minutes and think about this.

You can't give something that you don't have to others. How do you earn the respect of others? If we could master this, then we could considerately show respect to those who deserve it.

But not everyone deserves it. Not everyone in power, management, or in your company deserves respect. It does not come with a badge, rank or position. Respect is most definitely earned.

People think they have earned it so they think they deserve it, be it through tenure, longevity, birthright or ownership.

People also perceive respect as an external experience when it's really an internal one. If you can find something within that you are proud of, something that you have achieved, you will have a healthy level of self-love, and then you can find it in someone else. You will know where to look in others.

You do not have to like them, or everything they have done, but looking for the good in others will raise your awareness and you will find something you can respect about them.

Respect is an inside job. It starts with you. Self-respect is the starting point to respecting others.

Self-respect is the real recognition you deserve. Recognition leads to respect.

14. LOVE

Love life. Love your job. Love your customers.

Sounds simple. But it is a sad fact that not many people do. They work because they have to, not because they want to. They are in their job because that is what came along when they were searching for a new job and they are still there.

There are three facets to consider here: being more loving towards colleagues, being more loving towards yourself, while also loving what you do.

I think these are interrelated. It's hard to love yourself deeply if you don't like what you are doing on a daily basis. You would always be asking 'why' and demanding an answer. It is hard to love your colleagues, the people that are on this journey with you, if you are unhappy in any way with your lot.

To be more loving towards whomever, you must feel love for yourself. "Your cup hath to run over" before you can give it. Exactly like self-respect. You can't give away something you do not have.

You will be recognized and remembered for being more loving towards others, for treating them as they want to be treated, for spending time with them and showing an interest in them.

However, treating people in this way will not be sustainable unless you find it in you to do the same for yourself. So, we are back at the start again. To treat others well, you must first love yourself and love what you do.

The hard work is really in deciding what it is that you love to do. Then when you are doing what you love, it will not seem like work, and you can concentrate on looking after others and adding value to their lives. Whether you choose to be a nurse, a carpenter, a banker or a trainer, when we are absorbed by what we do for the right reasons, good things flow from it.

Introduce love into what you do and the recognition you want will be wrapped up in the responses you get from the people around you.

15. GRATITUDE

One simple way to start the process of learning about yourself, who you are, what you want, how you treat others and who you want to become is to start a gratitude log. Being grateful for something is a step towards showing gratitude to others.

Strangely a lot of people find it difficult to express themselves in a gratitude log. Maybe we take far too much for granted and in doing so expect that what we have is owed to us and is our given right.

With this in mind, remember to appreciate the small things that can make all the difference. If you feel you are owed a living by a company, it is hard to be thankful for the opportunities that present themselves.

In the book *The Science of Getting Rich,* Wallace Wattles writes that: "The entire process of mental adjustment and atonement can be summed up in one word, gratitude."

So when we feel out of sorts, or under pressure or someone has upset us, it is a first-step response to take stock and to refer to a gratitude log.

RECOGNITION PLAN
SECTION TWO

Building on the work from section one, now consider how you treat others and any changes you want to make to get the recognition you are aiming for.

Section	Where are you now?	Where do you want to be?	What will you do?
1 How You Are	Enthusiastic Cynical	Be seen to be enthusiastic Adopt a more positive approach	Speak up at the next team meeting about my new productivity idea Talk with colleagues about what is going well
2 How You Treat Others	Polite but don't really get involved	Be more helpful and interested in others	Arrange to go out with each of the team for a one-to-one coffee this month
3 What You Do			
4 How You Behave			

WHAT YOU DO

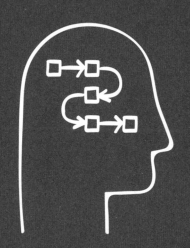

What you do speaks volumes. Small things can often make all the difference. Even doing nothing has an impact and not sending that text says a lot.

People may forget what we say, but they tend to remember the way we made them feel. This is often achieved by what we do.

16. CARE

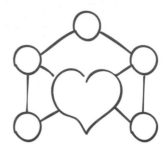

It's the attention to detail that separates the good from the great. To dot every 'i' and cross every 't' you need to care about what you do. You have to want to stand out. You have to want to be known for excellence.

Excellence comes as a standard. Set those standards high, hold yourself to them, never let them fall. Do not compromise. Compromise leads to mediocrity.

Ensure every piece of correspondence that leaves your possession reaches or exceeds these high standards. Do not take for granted that others will deliver the same as you. Read everything that goes out with your name on it.

The impression this approach leaves is a cumulative one, both good and bad. Be consistent. People will be watching, take my word for it.

Have you ever watched a movie where you have spotted something wrong with the continuity? Have you ever read a book where there is an obvious spelling mistake? One of your questions you ask yourself is: "How come? With all that effort and money spent they didn't see this?" It may not detract from the overall enjoyment of the film, but you'll be looking harder next time to spot errors.

Don't let simple errors or mistakes detract from your message. Be recognized for excellence. Take time to care, and care about your lasting impression.

Care too about your reputation. It takes time and effort to build and moments to shatter, particularly in this day and age of instant social media exposure. Reputations build confidence, so guard yours jealously.

Think before you post, so much can't be undone. Care what people think and people will think you care. And you do.

17. VOLUNTEER

Dangerous? Sometimes yes. This is truly a way to step up, stand out and get recognized. Volunteering for the right project at the right time can be a game changer in a quest to get the recognition you think you deserve.

It doesn't have to be a planet-saving mission; something as simple as washing the dishes in the office or making the tea first can score you major points.

Not making a fuss and quietly going about the task leaves a comfortable background effect that makes people feel easy. If done in a "look at me" kind of a way, it can result in a net loss in the brownie points league.

Consistency is important. Be reliable. Sporadic efforts leave people questioning your motives. But at the same time, be careful that people don't start to take this volunteering for granted. You should think these volunteering opportunities through to the end and beyond.

What seemed like a good idea at the time can soon turn into a chore.

How do you maintain the desired impact and keep it meaningful for you, the team, the employer, and the community?

Volunteering has to mean something and be of value: you need a plan. It has to deliver ultimate value because you have limited resources and you have to manage them, be they time, energy, finance or passion.

This can sound very pre-meditated and calculating, but it's important to think about all of this because next time you may be required to do even more.

This is where knowing what tasks are regular, routine and what the projects are that are coming down the line makes a difference. Saving yourself for the right moment could be key to getting that recognition that you think you deserve.

18. GET NOTICED

Sounds so simple, but is it?

It can be a lot easier to be noticed for doing the wrong thing, for being late, doing a poor job or not meeting a deadline. But being noticed positively for doing a good job on time to a high standard can be trickier than you think.

Therefore, you need to think about your personal impact. Most people don't think about this. Thinking about how to get noticed in the right way will put you ahead of the game.

First, don't be late, do a poor job or miss deadlines.

Let's keep this in context; this is about achieving the recognition you think you deserve. So if that task took a lot of time, brain power and persistence and you think it should be appreciated, what do you need to do to receive a "thank you"?

Of course, it all depends on the situation and the task. Let's take a simple task of processing an order form for instance. Assuming that you knew how to do it, this task may take you 20 minutes.

Then an extra simple step of emailing the customer to inform them that their order is underway or the sales person that their sale is in the system can have really positive consequences. This positive extra step in the sales process can create positive feedback and a confidence in you. Sometimes, just knowing that something is happening in the background makes customers or colleagues think they are getting good service.

Don't be 'a suck-up': balance this type of feedback with a need to know. The development of this small skill will be a good lesson for the future.

Make sure that you are known for completing a task, and think ahead to make the company look good as well as everyone involved in that process.

19. PARTICIPATE

"Don't be ridiculous!" you may say. Yes, of course we need to use our brains here. To be involved in absolutely everything at work is impossible. Fundamentally you should pick the 'key' things to participate in. To be deliberate, to do things on purpose, to do the things that fit into your evolving master plan, the things that get you noticed, the things that get you recognized.

It is important to note that it's not just doing these things that counts, you must do them well and with the right attitude.

Are you a Fire Marshall? First Aider? Project Leader? On the quiz team? It doesn't have to be much, but being involved gets you recognized.

Think about what you can help with, get into, that would at the same time be a strategic fit for your own development. This may not seem obvious at first, but if you look outside the box relevance can appear.

Testing the fire alarms every week may not seem the most exciting job, but it demonstrates reliability, an appreciation of subtle office workings and, in the end, reliability. Your reliability. You will be recognized as the one that quietly gets these things done.

Manning a company stand at a trade show may seem interesting or a bore at first (depending on your outlook) but the value may be hidden in plain sight. It's not just an opportunity to meet new customers, but also your competitors. Participating at that trade stand could be the one thing that gets you recognized on a much bigger stage than just the office.

So, of course, not every activity will be of use to you and fit strategically into your plan. Consider the goals of your plan, your strategy, your approach. If the activity fits in, do it. Look for the benefits beyond the task. You'll be glad you did and be recognized for it.

20. INCREASE RESPONSIBILITY

This is a difficult one. Some would say they can't do any more; some would say why should they do more? And some would say how much will I get for doing more?

All of these could be valid questions. It's contextual. A lot of people are doing just enough to be retained and a lot of companies are paying just enough to retain them. Quite a nice balance. What an opportunity.

Be the one that stands out and asks for more. Do it well, to get recognized. Sounds easy, but it's not. It takes a lot of planning, effort and organization.

There is a law of compensation. You are remunerated in direct proportion to:

1. **The need for what you do**
2. **How well you do it**
3. **The difficulty in replacing you.**

Figure it out. Do you think that taking on more would get you recognized? Possibly even better remunerated?

A lot of people end up with more responsibility by accident, by being available, by doing a good job, by being in the wrong place at the wrong time, but seldom by design. And usually they are not rewarded for it.

If you are not working to your own plan, you most certainly are part of someone else's. This rarely goes as well as you would have hoped.

So, when it comes to taking on more responsibility, do it on purpose. Once again, think it through, have a plan. Look beyond the edges.

"A man's vision must exceed his field of view." **Paul F. Warriner**

21. REPRESENT YOUR COMPANY

Sounds like a jolly? But not everyone sees it that way. A lot of corporate events are in the evenings or on the weekends. Certainly, you will need to travel. This may not be convenient for you. But as a business mentor once said to me, "If you're interested in something, you'll do what's convenient, if you are serious about something, you'll do what it takes."

I think that sums it up.

What is the upside of attending a company event? Meeting new customers, making new friends and contacts, visiting different places, experiencing a new culture. Seeing if your product really is the best. Making sure to be the perfect host, smiling and certainly acting as though you are on stage. Every moment counts. Every hand shake matters.

Putting yourself out there and participating with the right attitude will get you recognition. Once again, choose the right events, the ones that meet your criteria, as well as the company's. Be on purpose. Be like a top athlete and select the right tournaments to compete in.

Being recognized in this kind of arena can open so many doors. Maintain the new connections you make and expand your horizons and you literally have the whole world at your feet.

22. TRAIN OTHERS

You may have heard of the learning pyramid that was researched and created by the National Training Laboratories in Bethel, Maine? It relates to average retention rates. From traditional passive learning methods like attending a lecture, through to reading, audio visual to demonstration, retention increases from 5% to 30%. Participating in a discussion group increases your retention ability to 75%. But the most powerful way of retaining information is to teach what you know and immediately use what you have learned yourself.

This is a double whammy for those looking to build their credibility and get recognized. Help someone develop, teach them what you know or what they want to know. In doing so, you will learn and integrate your knowledge and skills on a deeper level and affect positive change in others.

Take the time to learn how to train others effectively, be a coach, be comfortable presenting and speaking to groups, as well as individuals.

Be like your favourite teacher, be remembered. That's recognition. You will experience more consistent moments of recognition when you add to people's work and lives. It's cumulative.

Put some time aside on a regular basis, maybe each day, or once a week or month, to teach someone. Train to gain. All of us have something to teach and experiences to share. Don't be shy; it's your duty. What a fantastic environment we would live in if everyone was looking to help and teach.

Of course, you have a day job, but put this in the roles and responsibilities; you'll be glad you did.

23. BE A MENTOR

You can take training to another level by sharing your experience. Add to the universal cumulative learning mind. Don't stop the flow of knowledge by holding on to it for just yourself. Give someone else the benefit of what you have learned.

You could mentor a colleague in your department, you could mentor a new starter in another part of the company or someone in a different company or even in another country!

Several things happen when this is done. First, it draws the best from you and forces you to present yourself from a completely different standpoint. It will help you develop yourself, because as a mentor you will be looking at the good, the bad, the losses and gains and packaging them in bite-sized learnings for someone else to digest. It's very reflective, can be very humbling and shows things about yourself that could be very useful for your own growth. Second, the mentored has a whole new perspective on their work, their efforts and their life. It will cause them to expand, feel wanted, feel as though someone else has an interest in them. Give them hope, encouragement. This new-found sense of feeling special and of pride will inevitably cause them to behave and perform differently.

Of course, that's the goal. But mentors are rarely trained as mentors. Just because you were once good at something, or are good at it, doesn't make you a good teacher, coach, manager or mentor.

Being a mentor requires commitment and dedication, because many times these good intentions go to pot. Mentors don't show up. Physically or mentally. They don't deliver, meetings aren't scheduled, or get cancelled.

Be excellent at it, take it seriously, have some pride in this huge opportunity. Don't be viewed as a mentor that doesn't show up, in whatever way. Get some training. You will be recognized immensely for this privilege if you do it well and speed up the flow of learning for others.

24. RUN MEETINGS EFFECTIVELY

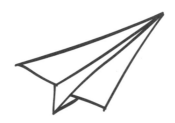

Wow, there is so much information out there on this, it's a whole book in itself. The point of this section is to focus your mind on what it means to you if you do this right.

Be punctual. Start on time. Set the standard. Have an agenda, manage it tightly. Only have those needed attend the meeting. Your respect for others' time and workload will be noted.

If it's not your meeting and it's poorly run, offer to chair the next one. Show them what a good meeting could look like.

Find a way, find what works.

If there is cloud-cuckoo thinking in your company and you have to attend endless, pointless meetings, then approach them with a different mindset. Work the room. Watch the people. Pay attention to the content, but observe others. Note their style, their behaviour, how they think. They are now under your microscope, examine as many aspects of your colleagues' behaviour as you can.

This alone will give you an advantage and help you learn to navigate the business landscape with much more ease.

Be known as a stickler for effective meetings. There are so many meetings happening each day: internal meetings, external meetings, sales meetings, management meetings, board meetings, client meetings, kick-off meetings, huddles, stand-up meetings, town-hall meetings, brain storms, those quick two-minute meetings and those two-day workshops we had better be getting a lot of value from. Make each meeting worthwhile.

But do we really need all of these meetings? Only have them if you need them. Be recognized for identifying the opportunity to increase productivity and release some capacity in people's lives to get on and do their jobs.

25. FOLLOW UP

This could so easily be focused on sales. But it applies to all aspects of work. So, follow up and not just once! Make sure you present your work and follow it through so that you know it has made a difference.

When you delegate, keep an eye on what was delegated; don't interfere, but check in. Stay informed, follow up.

Follow up on those action points from meetings. Make sure you review your notes and schedule the actions into your diary. Otherwise, you'll end up at the next meeting not having done all the tasks from the last one. The risk is of being known as never getting anything done and promising but rarely delivering.

The simple act of scheduling the tasks in your diary, not on a to-do list, can elevate your productivity enormously.

Follow-up in sales is vital. Not just in the moment of the sale, but in after-care too. Clients often want to feel part of something, so following up and asking if they are using the device, if all aspects of what they bought are working, or if that new car is in fact performing as promised, are important parts of cementing that relationship.

Following up is linked to completing and finishing. It's also linked to caring and consideration. Asking how someone is feeling once they return to work after having been ill is an example of follow up. It shows you care. Sending a 'good luck' text to someone about to deliver a major presentation can make all the difference.

Follow-up will lead to recognition. People will realize you don't just pay lip service to things, but that you like to know that what you did makes a difference.

26. DO YOUR THINKING ON PAPER

Much has been and can be said about this topic, particularly in the context of planning. Today you could replace the word paper with laptop or tablet, but I am a little old school.

Billions of pieces of information come to us every minute of the day. Our brain is a wonderful instrument as it filters out most of what we don't need in the moment and stores things for future reference. It links things together, creating neural pathways attaching them to experiences and feelings. We think in pictures and can recall these experiences and feelings quickly.

The point is, there's a lot going on inside our heads.

Give yourself a break, a chance to increase success by committing thoughts to paper. Get some of the information out of your head and into the physical realm, albeit with the intention of putting it back in there in a new, controlled format.

Putting it down on paper helps us recall, reference, order, plan, amend and develop ideas. It creates further capacity for you to be more creative, to visualize your thoughts on a deeper level. It will help you to share ideas so that others can benefit from them too.

Books are a good example of this. Where would all that great thinking be, if not on a bookshelf? Still inside someone's head.

Presenting your thoughts on paper gives you the opportunity to review them regularly, develop them and provides the chance to internalize them in a way that helps change habits and paradigms.

Writing down and reading your goals on a daily basis, perhaps first thing in the morning, at noon and before you go to bed, will help to reinforce them internally and find ways to take actions that bring them to fruition.

Literally writing how you would like to be recognized for the efforts you put in, coupled with the actions required, will help bring about that recognition.

So be careful what you think about. Think big, it takes no more effort to think of a million pounds than it does a thousand pounds. Be extra careful when you commit these thoughts to paper and take action. Magic happens!

27. GET QUALIFIED

The more you learn, the more you earn! Study all you can on the subject matter you're interested in. It matters. It matters to your clients, it will get you noticed by your peers and ultimately it will show up in your pay packet.

But more important than study and qualifications is application. Studying just to get the letters after your name has limited value. What you do with what you know and what you have learned is the key to real progress.

If you are making progress, you will be recognized.

Develop a study plan. What is the next recognized qualification you could attain? And the next one after that? Choose these qualifications well. The study plan should fit into your overall plan.

Specialize in something, there's riches in niches. It doesn't matter what your chosen field is, but aim to be the best you can be, through study and application.

Recognized qualifications speak volumes, and coupled with effective action they literally put the whole world at your feet.

Be prepared also to invest in your education. Take responsibility for your own development. Nobody is as affected by it as you, so own it. Make sure you get what you need. You may need to produce a business plan to get it, but it's worth it. After all, its business.

Qualifications are best deployed when you know what you want, what you want to do, but also what you want to achieve in the end.

28. STUDY AROUND THE SUBJECT

This follows on nicely from getting the right qualification you need to make an impact. Targeted study is important for rewards and credibility. Studying around the subject is important for that holistic approach to conversations, networking and general appeal.

Being recognized for being well informed is not only good for engagement at all levels; it opens doors and will get you invitations to otherwise closed events.

Being of pleasing character, good to talk to and having well-informed opinions will position you in the right place.

Once again it's going to require a study plan. Fit reading up on additional topics into the general plan. This may sound like hard work, but it forms a habit and habits form the person.

Make sure your habits are serving you well.

Read one book a week. You decide what the ratios are. You know where your focus needs to be. Reading numerous books will put you in the top few percent amongst others.

Malcolm Gladwell says in his book *The Outliers* that you need to study a subject for 10,000 hours to be an expert in it. You do the math. Studying around the subject adds variety and can often take you down roads that you otherwise would not have explored.

Once again, be the most informed you can be on your topic and those closely aligned to it. Be the one others turn to when they want to know something.

Become a speed reader, to help digest more information in less time. Read *Speed Reading* by Tony Buzan. Don't say you don't have time. Don't just read it through, study it, there's a world of difference. Master it, you will need to.

Studying around the subject will give you the edge and will help you impress on different fronts.

29. STAY RELEVANT AND CURRENT

Studying around the subject will almost certainly do this for you. It's important to study the right things at the right times. Just like studying for an exam, if you are looking at the wrong material you may not be well prepared. You know what you studied but you don't know how to answer the questions! Therefore, you're unlikely to pass.

What's relevant? Certainly news, current affairs, the latest papers within your industry, developments within your company and its competitors, be the one that knows all of this first, be an investigative journalist.

Use Google to alert you on a number of relevant topics, scan the trade mags and quality broad sheets. Set aside a block of time to do this on a daily basis. Make it a part of your daily routine, then it's a habit and you won't have to think about it.

How much time? Experiment, how fast can you read, scan? Back to that hugely important life skill, speed reading. Become a master of it.

Use technology and your creativity to do this. If you drive to work use this time and your car as a learning lab. Plug your earphones in if you commute by train or bus. Do this while on the treadmill in the gym, or while walking the dog. Schedule in the time, only then will it happen.

Use the tools and resources out there to make this easy, again it needs planning and organizing and practice. Executive summaries of books are great tools; they are called executive summaries for a reason.

As you get older and more advanced in your career, it can be difficult to stay competitive, relevant and useful. There is always a younger, more talented individual coming through. Work hard at staying up to date with all things that are important to your job, career and development, sometimes even if it's not of interest to you. It may be of interest to someone of influence around you.

30. DRESS WITH PRIDE

Tricky one this. There are many views. Here's mine.

Clothes are an expression of our personality, our feelings and moods. They say a lot, not all, but they do make an impression.

Use this to your advantage. Dress appropriately for every occasion. At work, wear what works. You could easily get recognized by wearing a banana onesie, however it is unlikely that this will be appropriate and it may get you recognition that you aren't looking for.

In the military people wear uniforms so everyone's the same. Likewise there are dress codes in banking, the NHS and factories, so it can be hard to stand out. However, the easiest thing to wear to help you stand out is a smile. In the biggest crowd, this will get you noticed. If it's genuine and consistent. this one small accessory is priceless.

In a world where most things are morphing to look similar, cars, lap tops, clothes, hair styles, this standing out from the crowd and getting recognized takes some thought. It may have already been done, there may be nothing new to do, to wear, to accessorize with. That's OK. Sometimes the simplest, most obvious things work best. Be genuine, be you.

If your business is precision, look precise, if it's creative, look creative. If your business is founded on order and systems, look orderly. All of these leave a lot of scope to personalize, but as usual there is often more to it than meets the eye.

31. HAVE A VISION, PLAN AND MISSION STATEMENT

Here we are at the nub of the whole book.

Have a vision: A vision for the job you are doing, the role you play, the future as you currently see it. What do your daily achievements look like? What is the recognition you are getting?

Have a plan: A plan of how to deliver this vision, to get this recognition, to get to your end game.

Have a mission statement of how you're going to live each day, and how you're going to behave to get the success you deserve.

I heard two colleagues talking the other day at a train station: "All I want is for 'them' to appreciate what I do, they must see it."

How many times have you said this, or at least thought it? Well the simple truth is that 'they' don't and 'they' don't have to. You have to take responsibility for your own success. You must recognize your own talents, strengths and give yourself the recognition, then you can go about getting it from others to advance your life.

If you do not have a plan, you will be part of someone else's. This invariably does not work out as well as you would have wanted.

But that's the point. There are very few people who have a plan in the first place. Most people don't give much thought to how they can step up, stand out and get the recognition they deserve. Sure, they may have a personal development plan as part of the appraisal system they are in, but how often does that get reviewed? Once a year at best.

Do you really want to be part of a system that you don't consciously influence? It's the subconscious that drives our daily habits and makes us who we are. But we have to sow the seeds, to design the track to run on. Or someone else will.

Your plan is hugely important, critical to your success. Like every good plan it will have milestones, KPIs, key deliverables, outcomes and time frames. Get one. Do it yourself or get help putting one together.

Recognition often validates what we do. But recognition has a much bigger part to play than validation: it's a building block to legacy.

It's our legacy that really makes the difference, and daily recognition is the fuel that keeps us going. But in order to really make an impact in the world, your work, your life, do everything on purpose, have a vision, get a plan, execute it daily and leave a legacy. Be recognized for this.

32. SET YOUR GOALS

Every new year millions of people start with New Year's resolutions and every day virtually everyone creates a to-do list, if only in their head! Very rarely do most people take the necessary steps to setting these goals out properly.

Why do we not succeed? Why do we not achieve our hopes and dreams?

Is it for want of motivation, commitment, will power, energy?

First, most people don't know what they really want. They might know what they don't want but they can't pin down what they truly do want.

Think about the recognition that you currently want at work, and in the future. Who do you want it from and what would be the outcome of this?

You might know that you don't want to be stuck in that job, or in that dull department, but what do you want to do instead of this and what kind of recognition will get you there?

Write it down. Those that do tend to be the ones that repeatedly achieve their goals.

Read this. At least three times a day. Morning, when you first get up, noon and the last thing at night before you go to bed. Make this a habit; it's critical.

Get emotionally involved with your answers. You need to be able to be excited by them. They have to mean something to you. This emotion has to filter through the protective crust we surround ourselves with and percolate down to stir your soul.

Use all available mediums to achieve this: words, pictures, sounds, smells, even tastes. Vision Boards too – more on these later.

Meditate. Relax, let these new dreams, thoughts and goals get through to the power house that drives your success, your subconscious.

Change your paradigm. Every day, take action to build new patterns, habits that serve you better. New habits that get you noticed, habits that get you the recognition you deserve and move you on to the goals you have set for yourself and your career.

This is not a one-off exercise. Goals change and develop, do not be frightened to set new ones when old ones are achieved. In fact, this is a vital key to continuous improvement, to self-actualization.

Do not underestimate the importance of taking action to achieve your goals. They won't just happen, no matter how hard you positively think about them. There is a lot of doing to do.

33. GET
A COACH

Although it may sound simple to have a vision and a plan, it's actually far from easy. This is where you need some guidance. Getting a coach is a great place to start.

There are many places to look to find the right person for you. This could be external or internal. This book may be one. Your manager may be able to coach you, another manager may be better. Often people are assigned a mentor or coach as part of their development plan. If you haven't been, ask about it and assess the options.

Many Human Resources (HR) people are tasked with delivering this kind of help. Once again, if you have an HR department, explore the options.

There are several things to consider when deciding on internal or external coaching resources. Each has their benefits. With internal coaching, these do understand the company, systems, environment and possibly you. This can be an advantage. Or it can be a disadvantage. External coaches are not influenced necessarily by the company, politics, the current systems and environment. They can be a lot more independent in the help and guidance that they offer.

These are important points to consider and depend on where you are, where you want to go and what you want to achieve. Take your time, experiment and evaluate. There are many styles and personalities, so find someone that is a fit for you. You will know when this happens.

One of the first steps in getting a coach is to recognize that you need one and then not to be frightened to ask for one. A lot of people have a reticence to ask for help. They may feel it's a sign of weakness, lack of capability and an inability to cope. It truly is the opposite. It can be a strong sign of self-awareness, character and desire.

Cost also needs to be taken into account as the spectrum is as varied as a rainbow and you also need to factor in the time you are investing and the opportunity losses or gains. Here an internal coach can provide flexible options. Do the best that you can with the resources that you have, this includes your money, so ask around, do your due diligence. Understand what you are getting for your investment and measure it to ensure you do.

Ultimately it boils down to the relationship you have with your coach, the trust that you build up and the belief that you have in each other and the journey you are on.

So, if you feel stuck, confused about the way forward, get some help, get a coach. They will offer a new perspective and hold you accountable for the actions you need to take to get where you want to go. It's a very rewarding experience when all things align. An experience that has the potential to change the course of your life forever. This one step will get you recognized.

34. MASTER BUSINESS TOOLS

What software packages do you use at work? What bespoke piece of kit sets your business apart from the rest in your field?

Whether it's Microsoft Word, Salesforce, Vimeo or a demonstration product, know it backwards, inside out, cover to cover. Be confident with your knowledge of the full workings of all the tools that you use to present your company and its services.

Not knowing how to pivot tables, pull that report or press that killer button that predicts the future can leave you vulnerable. You may never need to use it in the line of duty, but being able to pull it out of the hat when the occasion demands will put you in the lead.

Know the shortcuts that save time, know which tools work in what environments, practice till it's perfect before you need to perform. As ever, the preparation you put in will pay dividends.

The command of the tools you use does not have to be world-changing or mind-boggling. It could be as simple as knowing that pressing the 'b' on a keyboard during a PowerPoint presentation makes the screen go blank/black. This can impress and make you look super professional. At the time of writing, this worked, but don't take my word for it: try it.

Master the tools, the libraries, the buttons, be recognized for knowing what tools do what and what is best to use.

35. MASTER COMMUNICATIONS MEDIA

Need I say more? Apparently so. You may be able to sell, you may be able to present but have you mastered all the forms of communication? Are there gaps that you could plug?

You never know these days when you will be pulled into a different arena to perform. You should also be aware of your weaknesses. Being able to craft a good sales letter but not being able to read it in front of a crowd may let you down. Don't think the job is done once you have left the stage, your credibility will crumble if you can't back it up. Be sure to work on all of your weaknesses.

The phone is such an important tool these days, make sure it works for you. Master the use of it and know the mechanics. A weak telephone manner is like a weak handshake – it leaves a poor impression.

Pay particular attention to your voicemail message. Get this right, make sure it marries up with and is consistent with all your other communications. All too often this element is missed and detracts from the overall message you are sending. Practice this, listen to it, have others comment on it, re-do it. Make it an extension of who you are.

The same goes for when you leave a message. Be sure in what you want to say, don't waffle and do make people want to call you back. Chances are they won't if you are unclear and messy in your message leaving.

There are so many ways to present your message, your personal brand. The increased usage of social media, podcasts, even Instagram TV has everyone on standby when it comes to how we are perceived. These platforms provide ingenious ways of being recognized; some are intrusive, some are dangerous if mishandled, but all are out there, so you need to be aware of them.

Don't shy away, they are only tools to get the recognition you deserve, deploy them as you see fit and master them.

As these technologies change with time, it's important for you to know the tools in the locker, master them where you can and keep current with new ones as they emerge.

36. MAINTAIN A SENSE OF PERSPECTIVE

This is a must-have skill that will set you apart. In a crisis, and there will be many throughout your working life, when all around you are losing their heads, you need to have the ability to remain calm and keep things in perspective.

As James Allen said in his book *As a Man Thinketh*: "The strong calm man is always loved and revered. He is like a shade giving tree in a thirsty land or a sheltering rock in a storm."

The crises do not have to be huge, but people often lose sight of the big picture or what really matters. Stepping back from the brink and seeing things more clearly will give you a chance to step up and take the lead.

People can react badly to mistakes, losses or bad news. Be the one that sees it differently, a learning opportunity, or for what it really is, a chance to perform better. Re-frame things and spin them a new way. Your team will start to trust you and look to you when there are tough decisions to make or when angry clients turn up. That shade giving tree will look increasingly inviting.

Perspective pays dividends. It is all about seeing things differently from the rest. Swimming against the tide, bucking the trend. All made possible because someone is looking at a different picture, the bigger picture. Something other than what is in front of them, right now.

Right now, your career is at a certain point. This is a fact. Stand up, move across the room and look back at where you were sitting. Picture that person, what do you see? What would you say to them if they wanted to change? What can you see from this new place that they can't? What could they do differently to move out of a rut?

Practice this technique again and again. Imagine you are above the desk where you are working, looking down through a glass ceiling. How do you now see the desk, the tasks, the challenges?

This third-person view is a useful tool to help develop your perspective. You may see the steps to greater recognition a lot more clearly from across the room.

37. WIDEN YOUR VIEW

In the words of that budding author Paul F Warriner, "A man's vision must exceed his field of view." Now what did I mean when I crafted these words late on a Sunday night?

Not sure really; it was a long time ago, but I suppose I was musing that people usually aim for only what they can see, or what they know to be possible.

If we could see beyond the horizon, beyond our normal field of view, what would be possible?

What's the next breakthrough invention, what is the next step that makes our work easier or more fulfilling?

Accepting the status quo is settling for mediocrity. We are either growing or dying. Nothing is ever stationary or perfectly in balance. If we are not looking to improve, we are falling behind.

Widening your field of view could involve reading another book, attending another networking meeting or spending time shadowing a colleague in another department.

However you choose to widen your field of view, it will bring more opportunities into focus, and seeing them and taking advantage of them will gain you recognition and put you at the leading edge.

38. FIND SOMEONE WHO PLAYS AT WHAT YOU WORK AT

This is a concept that I came across while studying with John Assaraf, the personal development expert featured in the hit film *The Secret*.

Your skills, passion and strengths may lie in selling, but you hate paperwork. This concept suggests that you find somebody to do your paperwork, someone who loves doing paperwork and gets their kicks from seeing it done well.

Marketing is the life blood of any business, and there are a lot of ways to do this, too many for one person to master them all. Find the right people to do this for you and be recognized for leading them well.

Outsourcing should never mean abdication. Stay connected and involved and take responsibility and interest in the results. It's diffi-cult to outsource your way to recognition, but I am sure you can find ways to work with other people's strengths.

These concepts are all about leveraging yourself in the most efficient way. By sticking to what you know and what you do well, you give others space and opportunity to shine and step up to their plate.

A great way to achieve these improvements is to do more of what you love, less of what you tolerate and none of what you hate. A great goal to have and yet another concept I heard from John Assaraf.

A good question to keep asking yourself throughout the day is: "Is what I am doing moving towards or away from my goal?" Quite simply, either stop, delete or delegate that task. Avoid being a busy fool and concentrate on what is important.

RECOGNITION PLAN
SECTION THREE

Having looked closely at how you treat others and what you
wanted to change, now look at what you are going to do differently.

Section	Where are you now?	Where do you want to be?	What will you do?
1 How You Are	Enthusiastic Cynical	Be seen to be enthusiastic Adopt a more positive approach	Speak up at the next team meeting about my new productivity idea Talk with colleagues about what is going well
2 How You Treat Others	Polite but don't really get involved	Be more helpful and interested in others	Arrange to go out with each of the team for a one-to-one coffee this month
3 What You Do	Volunteer for a few things	Have this extra commitment recognized	Pick one project a month that has a big impact and look for two ways to leverage that immediately
4 How You Behave			

HOW YOU BEHAVE

How you choose to behave is the outward expression of who you are and what you have learned. You may know something intellectually but not be able to translate this into your behaviour, therefore there is always room to grow.

It is how you behave repeatedly that drives the results you get. Knowing something is good and acting on it will move you forward; repeating this positive behaviour creates the habits that makes us who we are.

39. BE PUNCTUAL

Time is Money - a saying you often hear.

Don't waste time, your most precious resource.

So, what about being punctual, how important is it to your success?

All I know is that I hate being late, I feel as though others who are habitually late have no respect for other people's time, therefore they have no respect for other people. Since time slips away so easily it needs to be treated as precious.

Notice the words there: hate, feel, slip, respect, precious. Emotive words. Not just for me, but for many others, maybe your boss. Ask anyone who's waited for a builder or telephone engineer!

Of course, time is important for success. How you treat it and use it in the context of yourself and others will definitely get you noticed.

Being noticed and being recognized do not necessarily mean the same thing! You could be noticed every time you are late (rarely if you are always early, one of those strange quirks!). You may get recognized for being punctual and for getting lots done in the time given.

So, what does being punctual mean?

To me it means thought, planning, consideration, order, urgency, importance, respect and recognition. It means that you recognize the value of your time and the time of others. But, if indeed it is the most precious resource we have, something that cannot be recreated or reused, why do we waste so much of it and abuse it? Because most people don't think, plan, consider others, have order in their lives, have a sense of urgency, have a sense of respect for others and indeed recognize the fact that time is precious.

Strangely the perception of time has changed, over time. It seems less fashionable to be punctual. We have the ability to muster a gathering in moments with technology, yet if someone is late beyond the vague boundaries of today's etiquette yet if someone is late it still annoys us!

Time is our greatest gift we should use it wisely. If you adopt these principles of time and punctuality you will be recognized and you will achieve more in your day and throughout your career.

Stand for something, recognize that your time, and other people's time, is important and is worth far more than money; once spent you can never get it back.

Be recognized for recognizing this truth, it will serve you well, over time and in this moment.

40. BE CONSTRUCTIVE

Sounds so easy. Is it really? Can any of us stop that inner critic from voicing an opinion that has the potential to deflate?

You may well be aware of the sandwich method when giving feedback: what was liked, what could have been better and what would have been desirable. Here the feedback concludes with a constructive suggestion of how to improve and be more on target (in someone else's view!). This method is intended to leave the individual focusing on the possibility of doing better rather than what didn't go so well.

A good intention. But it's a well-documented fact that any criticism at all has the potential to derail fragile egos. After all, isn't it the filling in the sandwich that we look for?

So being constructive is more a state of mind, a way of being. If you are always constructive in your approach, looking for the good, making simple uplifting comments that are well placed and trying consistently to leave an impression of improvement, then people can more readily deal with the negative, because they know there's always a positive. Being positive and constructive can go hand in hand. But they are not the same. Being constructive has a more incremental feel. Hence the building to a positive outcome.

Being constructive with yourself is a whole different thing. How do you silence that inner critic that chips away at your confidence, your self-esteem and your self-worth? If you are held back by critical self-talk, finding the flip side and being constructive is vital. This is where your journaling kicks in, where your gratitude log and recognition plan plays a key roles.

Know your successes, your strengths, the recognition you think you deserve and that which you get, map it out. Then use these anchors to build on and move forward when things are tough. After a bad day, look for the positives, look to be constructive and build new hope and desire for the future.

Be constructive with yourself about the efforts of your day. Give yourself the recognition you deserve and others will give it too.

Being constructive helps build people, teams, companies. It will help build your recognition.

41. GO THE EXTRA MILE

So much has already been written about the value of going the extra mile. I am sure it could be a book on its own. But it's true, it can make all the difference. Sure, the cynics will say you'll get taken for granted or taken advantage of, but there are often real gains to be made.

As in the gym, that extra push brings pain but also gain. Things change, things grow. Only when you push yourself beyond what you feel comfortable doing will you truly develop and have more to offer.

Jim Whittaker, the first American to summit Everest said in his book *Life On The Edge*: "If you're not living on the edge you're taking up too much space." Interesting. Think about this for a minute. There is far less traffic and congestion in that extra mile, purely because not many people are prepared to go there.

In a sales context, making an extra call, talking that quote over instead of posting it, sending a thank you note, can all pay untold dividends. In time, you will be able to tell exactly how much going this extra mile is worth to you. Record your effort, record the results, you will be amazed. Not only is there less traffic on this extra mile, there is more space to get noticed and ultimately make a difference.

What's your extra mile? Take five minutes and think about it. It may differ every day, but it will probably take less effort than you think.

So think about it, write it down, do it, measure it. You will then have a new metric to use: Gain per Extra Mile.

42. DEVELOP A PERSONAL STYLE

Personal style isn't just about the way you dress. It's so much more. It's about the way you behave, carry yourself, your attitude, your presence.

This is a hard one to articulate. Everyone knows when they meet someone with gravitas, with charisma, with style. They feel it, they sense it, they can't help but be drawn towards them.

If it were easy to bottle, it would sell by the boatload. But it's not. It can take years to define and refine this kind of style. Some try and never really succeed. The sooner you start on this particular mission, the more chance you have of perfecting it.

David Beckham has it, most footballers try but don't capture it! Bill Clinton has it, most politicians don't, most don't try!

It's everything about you, it's who you are at that moment in time. It's not one thing, and it's not the same thing, it's a combination of different things for everyone. But it is definitely something worth having.

Of course, you can have different styles and of course you can reinvent yourself at any time. Just look at David Bowie, each style different, each as appealing, each as successful. Notice how sports teams adapt their style of play to suit the opposition, often with the same players but always with a completely different mindset.

Perhaps that's it. It's a mindset. What you focus on internally finds a way of expressing itself externally. Be mindful about what you think, be purposeful about what you think about, but above all, think.

All to one aim, to enhance who you are and to gain that recognition you think you deserve.

43. WHEN TO LEAD

Stepping up, putting yourself in the firing line, putting your head above the parapet is a challenge. But this action will get you recognized. Companies are looking for people that can do this, but only a few are willing to chance it.

The reason is there in the word 'chance'. It can be a game of chance, stepping up and putting yourself out there. Not necessarily in your abilities, but in the reception you may get from the business, your colleagues and/or your clients.

Having a clear plan of what you are trying to achieve by leading from the front will mitigate the chance element of this action. If you are confident in your abilities, you are enthusiastic and you know what you want, then you can see whether this strategy pays off or not. Listening to the feedback and tweaking the approach will move you forward and ultimately get you noticed.

Leading a project, a campaign or an independent group can be tricky because of the variables and the uncertainty. If you have a plan and are doing things on purpose, there is less chance and more certainty.

Proper planning will take the fear out of these situations. The reaction you get, the results you achieve, are all part of the process and will help you do it better next time.

44. WHEN TO FOLLOW

Knowing which action to take comes with experience. Experience comes with having success and making mistakes. Experience will lead you to take more action.

Allowing someone to take the lead can be the right thing to do, supporting them on their journey can benefit you too. Being swept along by the flow of a river can carry you far, it is knowing when to jump in that often leads to new ways.

Following someone else on purpose allows you to observe their skills, behaviours and character. Learn from this. Learn what works and understand why.

Know when to stop being a passenger and when to start driving the bus. Because sometimes it's the bus that is recognized and not the driver, but at least be at the wheel to steer it your way.

45. BE A THOUGHT LEADER

Thoughts are who you are, they are what make you. Original thoughts are rare, the reorganization and new presentation of existing thinking is the usual. Nevertheless, it's invaluable. The repetition of new ideas in different formats help us integrate and use them. This is what this book is, a collection of current thinking and ideas presented in a new, digestible way to help you get the recognition you deserve.

Being a thought leader will do this too. It takes time, study, interest and dedication to a subject matter. All of which will pay dividends beyond the norm.

Have a thought, develop it and present it. Give it life. It could be on a process, an approach, a client, on a layout or venue. It doesn't have to be world-saving or life-changing.

But guess what! The more you practice, the more you exercise the thought leading muscle, the more your ideas will get bigger and better, the more impact they will have and the more you will be associated with that impact. As a result, you will get recognition.

Be brave. Externalize what you are internalizing. Particularly if it's on plan and moves you towards your goals. Random thoughts are good too, but grouped, purpose-driven ones will catapult you upwards.

Be creative. Thinking outside the box is powerful, but you should avoid being boxed-in in the first place.

Be agile. If you think, think fast. Implement.

Be calm. Be serene. James Allen wrote in his book *As A Man Thinketh*: "Calmness of mind is one of the beautiful jewels of wisdom."

Once upon a time, the mobile phone was just a thought. Now a healthy planet is just a thought. What's your legacy? What will you be recognized and remembered for?

Just a thought!

What will your thoughts lead to?

46. TAKE CONTROL

There is a problem today of expectation. People expect to be treated fairly, expect a pay rise, expect a good review. This is often accompanied with a blame attitude: it's the economy, the system, the management, clients. If we don't get what we expect, it is usually someone else's fault.

This external locus of control is a surefire way to build up negative stress in anyone's life. It is no wonder then many people are unhappy in their jobs.

Take control of your life, your achievements, the direction you go. Don't react to what happens to you; respond to it. Move towards an internal locus of control. Take back your life.

We all have a choice. We can all choose a path that serves us better. Jack Canfield in his book *The Success Principles* puts the decision to take responsibility for the outcomes in your life as a key factor in anyone's success.

Your bank account is what it is because of decisions you made. You are in the job you have because you chose it. The clients you serve are there for the same reason. If you want to change these things, you can. Just decide to do so and take responsibility for that action.

Own your life and be thankful that you can.

This can be hard to do, to step aside from a blame culture and separate yourself from a society that looks to attach responsibility to someone else.

Why are you where you are? How did you get there? Why aren't you getting the recognition you think you deserve?

Can someone else really make you unhappy, frustrated or disillusioned? Surely these are just responses you have chosen to adopt.

Stepping up, standing out and being recognized means taking control of your life. This mindset will be hugely liberating and a whole new world of possibilities will open up.

47. HAVE A CAN-DO ATTITUDE

You can draw on being positive, taking responsibility, always seeing the good in the situation and many more attributes mentioned in this book.

People want to work with and for someone with a can-do attitude. There is an energy around these positive people that attracts and demands the best from others.

If you are looking for job satisfaction and a sense of achievement then adopting a can-do attitude is a sure way to get it.

There are many examples where heroic efforts have changed the course of history. These are often as a result of people's can-do attitude. Many come from battles, many from medicine and many more from the various fields of human endeavour.

What heroic effort are you about to embark on? Just a small shift of attitude will be enough to change the course of your history.

Will it be spending a little more time with someone to work on their project, will it be looking a little closer for those hidden errors, will it be taking more care to get it right? Whatever it is, it will usually require digging a little deeper within yourself to find extra resources that set you apart from a mediocre effort and just doing enough to get by.

Most companies are paying people just enough to stop them leaving. But with a can-do attitude you can demonstrate the value you bring to those around you and the company, and as a result you could get paid what you are worth.

48. HAVE A SENSE OF HUMOUR

A lot of things will happen along the way, some good, some bad, some more memorable than others. Retaining your sense of humour will be vital if you are to keep your edge and keep moving forward.

How do you do that? Always remember the law of polarity. If something is really bad there must be something really good. Always be on the lookout for the good in everything and everyone.

As Monty Python said: "Always look on the bright side of life." I bet you whistled?

Having a sense of humour is not about telling jokes and messing around. It's about being able to see the funny side of things, to be able to laugh at yourself and the situation and not taking yourself too seriously. It's about maintaining a sense of perspective that keeps it all in balance when the day is done.

Maintaining a cheery and optimistic disposition has been proven to put you on the front foot when trying to get ahead. People would rather be around, mix with and work with colleagues who are upbeat and smiling than those who are frowning and unhappy.

It takes more energy to frown than to smile and let's not forget, a smile in return is perhaps all the recognition that you are looking for.

If your sense of humour is not your strong point and needs development, don't hold back, join in with others and laugh as much as you can. It's a great tonic and is proven to reduce stress and release those feel-good chemicals within us that we are all trying to find.

Pick a joke, a recent one, learn how to tell it well. Practice this until you could deliver it at the Palladium. The opportunity will present itself soon enough. If it is not your natural style, but you bowl others over with one or two good deliveries, you will win their hearts and be recognized.

49. BE THERE, BE PRESENT AND FULLY ENGAGED

Being present, being in the room, there are many ways to express this. But when you are not paying full attention, people notice, they can tell when you are not concentrating and your mind is elsewhere. It is disrespectful and rude, often not deliberate and with so much going on in people's lives, it's easy to understand that it can happen.

It amazes me how many people do a great job whilst at the same time they have negative stuff going on in their personal life. Work may provide an escape or sanctuary from all the other pressures in their life. They need to be recognized for achieving this.

When you love what you do, it seems so natural to be present, there, fully engaged. But when you are struggling to move towards your goal, it can be hard. So, this is where your plan is key. Focus on the results that you are after.

Remember Dale Carnegie's expression: "Act enthusiastic and you'll be enthusiastic." Act as if you are, until you are.

Act as if you are focused. Act as if you are interested and engaged. You can literally act yourself into the room.

50. BE COMMITTED AND DECISIVE

Following through on any plan takes commitment. Be it a diet, a business plan or recognition plan. Commitment is that inner resolve that comes from knowing what to commit to. It's a way of behaving that lets everyone know you are serious about an intent.

Only 100% will do. You can't be 99% vegetarian because people will not take you seriously.

Identifying where to focus this inner strength, this way of behaving is the key. Decide what to commit to and do it. Then it's done. If you decide to give up chocolate, it's done. To make a decision means to cut off all other options. If you really make a decision your commitment will show up and support that decision. If this means a lot to you, you will not falter. Have belief in yourself.

Make it easy for yourself, give yourself every chance you can to succeed. Stop buying chocolate, pay at the pump for your fuel rather than in the kiosk to remove the temptation to snack.

If you decide to apply for a new position, commit to that decision, go all out and do whatever it takes to get it. Only 100% is required. Then you will know you gave it your all, you did your best.

Nobody will ask for more, not even you. You are probably your own worst critic, silence that inner critic and celebrate your freedom. It is hugely liberating to make a firm decision and know that you don't have to keep looking backwards.

Look forward to the recognition you want and deserve by deciding to follow these ideas and commit to being all you can be.

In the words of the Na'vi from the film *Avatar*: "I see you".

RECOGNITION PLAN
SECTION FOUR

At this stage you have looked at how you are, how you treat others and the actions you need to take to change things. Now, what habits do you start to develop and how do you behave to make these plans stick?

Section	Where are you now?	Where do you want to be?	What will you do?
1 How You Are	Enthusiastic Cynical	Be seen to be enthusiastic Adopt a more positive approach	Speak up at the next team meeting about my new productivity idea Talk with colleagues about what is going well
2 How You Treat Others	Polite but don't really get involved	Be more helpful and interested in others	Arrange to go out with each of the team for a one-to-one coffee this month
3 What You Do	Volunteer for a few things	Have this extra commitment recognized	Pick one project a month that has a big impact and look for two ways to leverage that immediately
4 How You Behave	Often late for meetings	Be at meetings in advance properly prepared having done all the actions and read all the back-ground material	Organise diary to allow me to get to meetings five minutes early. Schedule time at the end of each day to review meetings and diarize time to complete actions. Use next week's sales meeting to practise new approaches.

Now go get recognized!

CONCLUSION:

A RECOGNITION JOURNEY

Probably the best way to draw this book to a conclusion is to tell a story about a client that embarked on this journey with me and although we did not know it at the time, we were following these steps.

My client Norman was employed at a small independent financial-services practice within a larger national firm.

At the time we started this journey, he was working from a small office, processing his own work and had a small but stable set of clients. He had a good reputation and had been in the industry for more than a decade. He had been in a failed business partnership and recently moved out from working at home.

For obvious reasons this story concentrates on his business transformation and the way he stepped up and changed and received the recognition he has today.

Taking on a coach was not a new thing, he had tried it before, it had kind of worked but he had not stuck to it for various reasons. He had plenty of tools, plenty of resources and lots of skill but was not using any of them well.

The one thing that stood out at the start was he had a burning desire to hit a certain company target that he felt would gain him the recognition he wanted and thought he deserved.

We went to work.

Over the next few months we put together a plan using the framework outlined in this book. We took massive action on a daily basis, we held each other accountable for delivering on steps within that plan and we grew to know each other well.

As a coach, there are many things you can teach, some things you can influence and steer but there are also many things you can learn from clients. This certainly happened. In facilitating this change and steps towards more recognition for Norman I noticed changes in myself.

A win-win situation.

Others benefited too, so things were moving in the right direction.

He focused on who he was as a person and turned his inner qualities into strengths and core values for him and for his business. He treated people better, clients, staff, professional colleagues and others within his wider business. He identified how people wanted to be treated, some differently from others, and he delivered on this in a very genuine way.

Things started to happen, business grew, he took on staff and moved offices twice. Locally his reputation was growing, within the wider company his head was above the parapet for the right reasons and people were starting to ask good questions. Bigger and better clients were coming along and that elusive target from the past looked doable now. He was starting to believe in himself.

Not everything went well all of the time, but each challenge was met with professional curiosity, i.e. what can I learn from this? And it was always put into the context of the master plan. It was the goal and the plan that kept him focused and driven. He knew if he kept on doing the things that worked each day, the clients would come, the business would grow and that recognition from all concerned would be there.

In short, he blitzed the first year's target and delivered on his plan. He certainly got noticed and was recognized for having achieved a breakthrough. He drew from himself the qualities needed to do so, he identified new ones to help him do better. He learned the daily steps to keep motivated, to have a work-life balance, to keep clients happy, staff happy, the family happy and himself happy.

And importantly he celebrated this success, this recognition, with his family. Ultimately the most important thing to him.

With this new-found recognition and change came responsibilities and different challenges. Having had a number-one selling album could he follow it up with another hit?

I am pleased to say he did. Over the next five years he moved offices twice more, he built a highly motivated, professional team, loyal to him and his values and their clients. Each year brought new goals and new challenges in a more regulated market than ever. Each one of these was dealt with in the team's stride but always in view of the plan. Each goal was met and celebrated.

Things continued to grow and develop as did his reputation and the recognition he received from those around him.

More than five years on, we are still working together. He continues to set ambitious goals, build plans and draw out the best from himself and his team. He knows more about himself than he ever did, the good and the not so good. He knows how these factors help or hinder him. He knows his personal impact on others and how to change this to get the results he wants. He knows the routines and activities that make a difference for him, his business and his family. And he knows the behaviours and habits that make for a fulfilling life.

The key learning for Norman from this recognition process was that no-one does it on their own. Everybody needs a little help along the way. Recognizing this and asking for help is a key step in the success journey. Having a plan and following it, even though it may change a little, is important too. Achieving the recognition you deserve and have worked hard for is no accident. Success and recognition happen by design; they are the effect of taking appropriate action. This recognition positions you for the next few steps and the next challenge to gain more. Recognition can be like a drug – the more you get, the more you want. Channel this well and the sky is your limit.

A key learning for me was the fact there is an immense amount of joy and reward in seeing others achieve their goals and get their recognition. You do not have to be in the spotlight to shine and be appreciated.

I am proud to have been a part of his journey of recognition and, looking back, to have drawn from it some of the inspiration for this book.

I am confident that if you follow some of the steps in this book, try some of the ideas out and experiment and find what works for you, that you will get the recognition you want and deserve.

It would be an honour to be part of your journey of recognition. I invite you to write to me and share your stories of recognition, the challenges you have and the new things that work for you so that we may share them and help others on their way.

It feels great to be recognized for something you have done, but guess what? It feels even better to recognize others for what they have achieved and to be able to show it.

FURTHER READING

Think and Grow Rich, Napoleon Hill

The Success Principles, Jack Canfield

As A Man Thinketh, James Allen

Spike, Rene Carayol

Start with Why, Simon Sinek

Maximum Achievement, Brian Tracy

You Were Born Rich, Bob Proctor

Seeds of Greatness, Denis Waitley

Ishmael, Daniel Quinn

What to Say When You Talk To Yourself, Shad Helmstetter

The Power of Now, Eckhart Tolle

The Chimp Paradox, Prof. Steve Peters

ABOUT THE AUTHOR

PAUL F. WARRINER is a well-respected coach, trainer and consultant with a wide range of experience both as an employee and entrepreneur. Over the last decade or so he has been successfully coaching and training sales teams, management teams, business owners and individuals alike to be their best.

Being the best that you can is much more than being good at your job or what you do. Through his work with these individuals, companies large and small, he has realized that even if you are at the top of your game you don't always get the recognition you deserve.

This led Paul to start the highly acclaimed blog *The Recognition Code* and develop the principles that make up this, his first book.

An engaging and inspirational speaker he believes that everyone deserves recognition and takes this message to the world through his work and interactions with clients.

Education does much, but encouragement achieves much more. Paul has encouraged hundreds of people to be their best and claim the recognition they deserved.

Sharing knowledge since 1993

- 1993 Madrid
- 2008 Mexico DF and Monterrey
- 2010 London
- 2011 New York and Buenos Aires
- 2012 Bogotá
- 2014 Shanghai